Francis Frith's
AROUND IPSWICH

◆

PHOTOGRAPHIC MEMORIES

Francis Frith's
AROUND IPSWICH

◆————————◆————————

Clive Tully

FRITH
BOOK CO

First published in the United Kingdom in 2000 by
Frith Book Company Ltd

Hardback Edition 2000
ISBN 1-85937-133-7

Paperback Edition 2001
ISBN 1-85937-424-7

British Library Cataloguing in Publication Data

Francis Frith's Around Ipswich
Clive Tully

Frith Book Company Ltd
Frith's Barn, Teffont,
Salisbury, Wiltshire SP3 5QP
Tel: +44 (0) 1722 716 376
Email: info@frithbook.co.uk
www.frithbook.co.uk

Printed and bound in Great Britain

AS WITH ANY HISTORICAL DATABASE THE FRITH ARCHIVE IS CONSTANTLY BEING CORRECTED AND IMPROVED
AND THE PUBLISHERS WOULD WELCOME INFORMATION ON OMISSIONS OR INACCURACIES

CONTENTS

FRANCIS FRITH: *Victorian Pioneer*

FRANCIS FRITH, Victorian founder of the world-famous photographic archive, was a complex and multitudinous man. A devout Quaker and a highly successful Victorian businessman, he was both philosophic by nature and pioneering in outlook.

By 1855 Francis Frith had already established a wholesale grocery business in Liverpool, and sold it for the astonishing sum of £200,000, which is the equivalent today of over £15,000,000. Now a multi-millionaire, he was able to indulge his passion for travel. As a child he had pored over travel books written by early explorers, and his fancy and imagination had been stirred by family holidays to the sublime mountain regions of Wales and Scotland. 'What a land of spirit-stirring and enriching scenes and places!' he had written. He was to return to these scenes of grandeur in later years to 'recapture the thousands of vivid and tender memories', but with a different purpose. Now in his thirties, and captivated by the new science of photography, Frith set out on a series of pioneering journeys to the Nile regions that occupied him from 1856 until 1860.

INTRIGUE AND ADVENTURE

He took with him on his travels a specially-designed wicker carriage that acted as both dark-room and sleeping chamber. These far-flung journeys were packed with intrigue and adventure. In his life story, written when he was sixty-three, Frith tells of being held captive by bandits, and of fighting 'an awful midnight battle to the very point of surrender with a deadly pack of hungry, wild dogs'. Sporting flowing Arab costume, Frith arrived at Akaba by camel seventy years before Lawrence, where he encountered 'desert princes and rival sheikhs, blazing with jewel-hilted swords'.

During these extraordinary adventures he was assiduously exploring the desert regions bordering the Nile and patiently recording the antiquities and peoples with his camera. He was the first photographer to venture beyond the sixth cataract. Africa was still the mysterious 'Dark Continent', and Stanley and Livingstone's historic meeting was a decade into the future. The conditions for picture taking confound belief. He laboured for hours in his wicker dark-room in the sweltering heat of the desert, while the volatile chemicals fizzed dangerously in their trays. Often he was forced to work in remote tombs and caves where conditions were cooler. Back in London he exhibited his photographs and was 'rapturously cheered' by members of the Royal Society. His reputation as a photographer was made overnight. An eminent modern historian has likened their impact on the population of the time to that on our own generation of the first photographs taken on the surface of the moon.

VENTURE OF A LIFE-TIME

Characteristically, Frith quickly spotted the opportunity to create a new business as a specialist publisher of photographs. He lived in an era of immense and sometimes violent change. For the poor in the early part of Victoria's reign work was a drudge and the hours long, and people had precious little free time to enjoy themselves.

Most had no transport other than a cart or gig at their disposal, and had not travelled far beyond the boundaries of their own town or village. However, by the 1870s, the railways had threaded their way across the country, and Bank Holidays and half-day Saturdays had been made obligatory by Act of Parliament. All of a sudden the ordinary working man and his family were able to enjoy days out and see a little more of the world.

With characteristic business acumen, Francis Frith foresaw that these new tourists would enjoy having souvenirs to commemorate their days out. In 1860 he married Mary Ann Rosling and set out with the intention of photographing every city, town and village in Britain. For the next thirty years he travelled the country by train and by pony and trap, producing fine photographs of seaside resorts and beauty spots that were keenly bought by millions of Victorians. These prints were painstakingly pasted into family albums and pored over during the dark nights of winter, rekindling precious memories of summer excursions.

THE RISE OF FRITH & CO

Frith's studio was soon supplying retail shops all over the country. To meet the demand he gathered about him a small team of photographers, and published the work of independent artist-photographers of the calibre of Roger Fenton and Francis Bedford. In order to gain some understanding of the scale of Frith's business one only has to look at the catalogue issued by Frith & Co in 1886: it runs to some 670

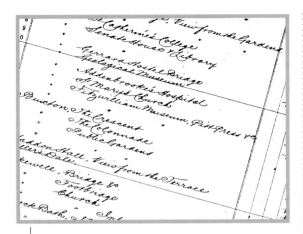

pages, listing not only many thousands of views of the British Isles but also many photographs of most European countries, and China, Japan, the USA and Canada – note the sample page shown above from the hand-written *Frith & Co* ledgers detailing pictures taken. By 1890 Frith had created the greatest specialist photographic publishing company in the world, with over 2,000 outlets – more than the combined number that Boots and WH Smith have today! The picture on the right shows the *Frith & Co* display board at Ingleton in the Yorkshire Dales. Beautifully constructed with mahogany frame and gilt inserts, it could display up to a dozen local scenes.

POSTCARD BONANZA

The ever-popular holiday postcard we know today took many years to develop. In 1870 the Post Office issued the first plain cards, with a pre-printed stamp on one face. In 1894 they allowed other publishers' cards to be sent through the mail with an attached adhesive halfpenny stamp. Demand grew rapidly, and in 1895 a new size of postcard was permitted called the

court card, but there was little room for illustration. In 1899, a year after Frith's death, a new card measuring 5.5 x 3.5 inches became the standard format, but it was not until 1902 that the divided back came into being, with address and message on one face and a full-size illustration on the other. *Frith & Co* were in the vanguard of postcard development, and Frith's sons Eustace and Cyril continued their father's monumental task, expanding the number of views offered to the public and recording more and more places in Britain, as the coasts and countryside were opened up to mass travel.

Francis Frith died in 1898 at his villa in Cannes, his great project still growing. The archive he created continued in business for another seventy years. By 1970 it contained over a third of a million pictures of 7,000 cities, towns and villages. The massive photographic record Frith has left to us stands as a living monument to a special and very remarkable man.

Frith's Archive: *A Unique Legacy*

FRANCIS FRITH'S legacy to us today is of immense significance and value, for the magnificent archive of evocative photographs he created provides a unique record of change in 7,000 cities, towns and villages throughout Britain over a century and more. Frith and his fellow studio photographers revisited locations many times down the years to update their views, compiling for us an enthralling and colourful pageant of British life and character.

We tend to think of Frith's sepia views of Britain as nostalgic, for most of us use them to conjure up memories of places in our own lives with which we have family associations. It often makes us forget that to Francis Frith they were records of daily life as it was actually being lived in the cities, towns and villages of his day. The Victorian age was one of great and often bewildering change for ordinary people, and though the pictures evoke an impression of slower times, life was as busy and hectic as it is today.

We are fortunate that Frith was a photographer of the people, dedicated to recording the minutiae of everyday life. For it is this sheer wealth of visual data, the painstaking chronicle of changes in dress, transport, street layouts, buildings, housing, engineering and landscape that captivates us so much today. His remarkable images offer us a powerful link with the past and with the lives of our ancestors.

TODAY'S TECHNOLOGY

Computers have now made it possible for Frith's many thousands of images to be accessed almost instantly. In the Frith archive today, each photograph is carefully 'digitised' then stored on a CD Rom. Frith archivists can locate a single photograph amongst thousands within seconds. Views can be catalogued and sorted under a variety of categories of place and content to the immediate benefit of researchers. Inexpensive reference prints can be created for them at the touch of a mouse button, and a wide range of books and other printed materials assembled and published for a wider, more general readership - in the next twelve months over a hundred Frith local history titles will be published! The

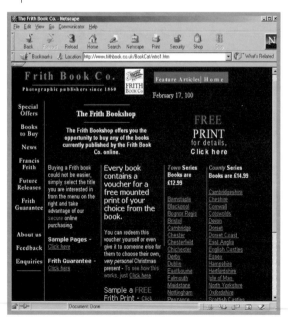

See Frith at www. frithbook.co.uk

day-to-day workings of the archive are very different from how they were in Francis Frith's time: imagine the herculean task of sorting through eleven tons of glass negatives as Frith had to do to locate a particular sequence of pictures! Yet the archive still prides itself on maintaining the same high standards of excellence laid down by Francis Frith, including the painstaking cataloguing and indexing of every view.

It is curious to reflect on how the internet now allows researchers in America and elsewhere greater instant access to the archive than Frith himself ever enjoyed. Many thousands of individual views can be called up on screen within seconds on one of the Frith internet sites, enabling people living continents away to revisit the streets of their ancestral home town, or view places in Britain where they have enjoyed holidays. Many overseas researchers welcome the chance to view special theme selections, such as transport, sports, costume and ancient monuments.

We are certain that Francis Frith would have heartily approved of these modern developments, for he himself was always working at the very limits of Victorian photographic technology.

THE VALUE OF THE ARCHIVE TODAY

Because of the benefits brought by the computer, Frith's images are increasingly studied by social historians, by researchers into genealogy and ancestory, by architects, town planners, and by teachers and schoolchildren involved in local history projects. In addition, the archive offers every one of us a unique opportunity to examine the places where we and our families have lived and worked down the years. Immensely successful in Frith's own era, the archive is now, a century and more on, entering a new phase of popularity.

THE PAST IN TUNE WITH THE FUTURE

Historians consider the Francis Frith Collection to be of prime national importance. It is the only archive of its kind remaining in private ownership and has been valued at a million pounds. However, this figure is now rapidly increasing as digital technology enables more and more people around the world to enjoy its benefits.

Francis Frith's archive is now housed in an historic timber barn in the beautiful village of Teffont in Wiltshire. Its founder would not recognize the archive office as it is today. In place of the many thousands of dusty boxes containing glass plate negatives and an all-pervading odour of photographic chemicals, there are now ranks of computer screens. He would be amazed to watch his images travelling round the world at unimaginable speeds through network and internet lines.

The archive's future is both bright and exciting. Francis Frith, with his unshakeable belief in making photographs available to the greatest number of people, would undoubtedly approve of what is being done today with his lifetime's work. His photographs, depicting our shared past, are now bringing pleasure and enlightenment to millions around the world a century and more after his death.

AROUND IPSWICH – *An Introduction*

MANY PEOPLE TEND to draw a comparison between Ipswich and Norwich as the major towns in their respective counties. If nothing else, an East Anglian derby match between Norwich City and Ipswich Town football clubs excites far more local passion than if either team were playing Manchester United! Although both towns are founded on ancient communities, Ipswich is more important than Norwich as a port - and indeed, it always has been. It is situated at the point where the freshwater River Gipping joins the head of the tidal Orwell Estuary, and even as far back as the 7th century Ipswich was not merely a trading port, it was the biggest in the country. Known then as Gippeswic, this Anglo-Saxon port survived many Viking raids. It very quickly established itself as a place of industry, producing a distinctive grey type of pottery which we know was widely distributed, both throughout East Anglia and beyond. It is very likely that the close proximity of the East Anglian royal palace at Rendlesham had a marked bearing on the fortunes of the town, as much trade in imported fine wines, furs and textiles passed through here, as well as the products of the local industry being sent

from here to other ports along the coast.

By the time of the Conquest, Ipswich had its own mint, and by the beginning of the 13th century the town's status was confirmed with its first charter, awarded by King John. The middle ages saw the town prosper through the East Anglian wool trade, and by the 17th century, there was also a thriving ship-building industry using Suffolk oak, with shipyards lining the banks of the Orwell. Indeed, in 1614, Ipswich was quoted as having more shipwrights than any port in England. In Georgian times, the town suffered a commercial decline, but its prosperity was restored by the Industrial Revolution, evidenced by the large number of 19th century houses in the town. Engineering businesses like Ransomes established themselves, producing everything from railway equipment to agricultural machinery.

But at the end of the 18th century, the most pressing problem was with the docks, where large ships were unable to berth. The river was silting up, and even at high tide it was becoming impossible to get upstream. The solution, which took another forty years, was to construct the Wet Dock by isolating a bend in the river and diverting the river itself into a bypass channel known as the New Cut. With lock gates to control access to it, the Wet Dock provided the means for ships to be able to dock at any state of the tide - at the time, it was the largest such enclosed area of water in Europe. Further improvements were made to the dock, but by the end of the First World War, the port had expanded beyond the Wet Dock - the river had been dredged and quays built to accommodate large ships. Ships do still unload in the Wet Dock, but increasingly it is being taken over by yachts and pleasure boats, while the cargo vessels unload at the riverside quays - the oil and grain terminals on the east bank, and the container and roll-on roll-off berths on the west.

The railway arrived in Ipswich in 1846, and with that came further expansion and improvements to the town's prosperity. However, it was not until 1860 that a tunnel was cut through Stoke Hill, thus enabling the

ST STEPHENS LANE 1921 70391

line to be continued to Bury St Edmunds and Norwich.

The basic street pattern of the town centre is still that of the medieval town, including a fine range of buildings dating from the 15th century onwards. Like Norwich, Ipswich was once surrounded by a wall, a legacy of which can be found in many of the street names, such as Westgate and Northgate. Cornhill, with its flamboyant mock Italian and Jacobean-style buildings, is on the original site of the market place of the town; it was also the place where several 'heretics' were burned at the stake. One block away is the Buttermarket, which contains the town's most famous building, the Ancient House. Also known as Sparrowe's House, this remarkable building is over five hundred years old; the walls of its upper floors, with their bay windows, overhang the lower part. Its interest lies in the elaborate moulded plasterwork designs on its outer walls - it is probably the best surviving example of pargetting in Britain. The panels below the first floor windows represent the continents of the known world at that time - Europe, Asia, Africa and America - along with the arms of Charles II (who, it is said, hid here after the Battle of Worcester) over the main doorway.

Just to the west is the Unitarian Meeting House, built about 1700. Inside, four great wooden pillars, said to be from ships' masts, form part of the structure, while the carved pulpit is quite probably the work of Grinling Gibbons. It is likely that this building was one of the first purpose-built non-conformist chapels, the Toleration Act having been passed only ten years previously. On the corner where St Nicholas Street is joined by Silent Street stands a magnificent group of Tudor houses with a carved corner post. Cardinal Wolsey is reputed to have been born in this area, and a plaque on one of the houses commemorates this. Nearby is Wolsey's Gate, the only surviving part of Cardinal Wolsey's ambitious plan to build a College of Cardinals. The building was started in 1527, and would have been quite extensive. But Wolsey fell from grace when he failed to support Henry VIII's wish to marry Anne Boleyn, and it was never completed. The brick gateway, with its barely discernible royal cipher, is all that remains.

Just a few years later, Christchurch Mansion was built on the site of the 12th century priory of the Holy Trinity. This Tudor country house is now a museum, and its adjoining art gallery houses a fine collection of paintings by Constable and Gainsborough. It is interesting to recall that this marvellous house almost became a housing estate in the late 19th century. The Cobbold brewing family bought the building and then presented it to the town, thus enabling us still to enjoy this monument to gracious living.

Tavern Street contains the Great White Horse Hotel, which, despite its Georgian facade, is a timber-framed building dating back to the 16th century. Famous visitors have included Dickens (who wrote about it in Pickwick Papers), George II in 1736, Louis XVIII of France in 1807, and Lord Nelson in 1800. Opposite the hotel stands a group of buildings which appear to be Tudor, but are in fact reproductions, built in the 1930s when such imitations were in vogue. Today, despite the presence of the two major ports of Harwich and Felixstowe only ten miles away at the mouth of the Orwell, Ipswich remains an important industrial and commercial centre.

THE ANCIENT HOUSE 1921 70399
On the corner with St Stephens Lane stands the Ancient House, a remarkable building which is probably the best surviving example of medieval pargetting - decorative plasterwork - in Britain.

THE ANCIENT HOUSE 1893 32205
When this photograph was taken, the richly pargetted Ancient House, which dates back to medieval times, was occupied by Fred Pawsey, selling books and stationery.

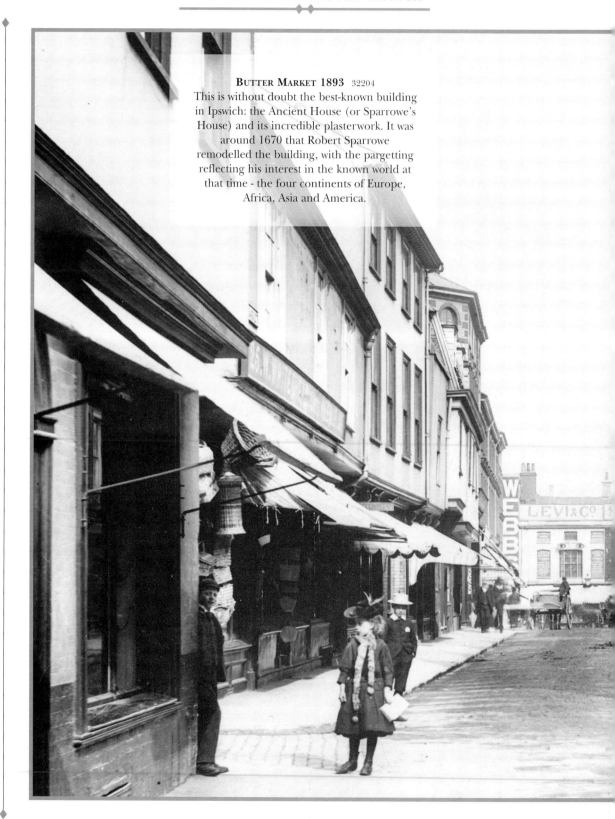

BUTTER MARKET 1893 32204
This is without doubt the best-known building
in Ipswich: the Ancient House (or Sparrowe's
House) and its incredible plasterwork. It was
around 1670 that Robert Sparrowe
remodelled the building, with the pargetting
reflecting his interest in the known world at
that time - the four continents of Europe,
Africa, Asia and America.

THE ANCIENT HOUSE c1955 118017

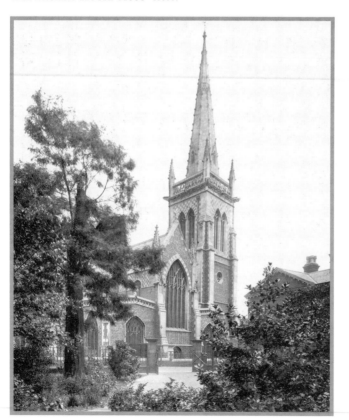

THE ANCIENT HOUSE c1955
Another view showing the elaborate
pargetting which has made the Ancient
House recognised as one of the prime
examples of its kind. At the cinema next
door, 'Easter Parade' is enjoying yet
another re-run, with seats priced at 2/9
and 3/6 (14p and 17 ½p).

ST MARY LE TOWER 1921
This medieval church, for many years
Ipswich's principal parish church, gave
its name to Tower Street. The original
spire collapsed in 1661, victim of a
hurricane which swept across the town.

ST MARY LE TOWER 1921 70402

ST STEPHENS LANE 1921 70391

It is three years after World War I, and a packet of ten Wills cigarettes can be bought in this tobacconists for 3d (three old pence). The newspapers are full of the news of the impending strike by the miners. Prime Minister Lloyd George had strikes by the miners, railwaymen and many others broken by troops and the use of emergency powers.

BUTTER MARKET 1921 70404
Up until 1810, Ipswich's Buttermarket was indeed the
scene for the sale of butter and other products. At this
time, it is one of the main shopping streets in the
town. At the far end on the left is the Ancient House,
with its unmistakable overhanging upper storey.

BUTTER MARKET c1955 I18006
Sturdy bicycles abound in this post-war view. But now, with increasing recognition that cars and pedestrians do not mix, the road sports a pedestrian crossing.

WOLSEY'S BIRTHPLACE, SILENT STREET c1955 I18047
On the corner of Silent Street and St Nicholas' Street we see this impressive group of Tudor buildings with a carved corner post. Cardinal Wolsey is reputed to have been born here.

THE HOSPITAL 1893
The East Suffolk Hospital was founded in 1835, starting out as a two-storey building. It was extended upwards in 1869, and a children's wing was added some five years later.

◆

THE HOSPITAL 1921
This photograph may not be entirely successful in posing people in front of the hospital building! It was taken just under a quarter of a century after photograph No 32216, and the creepers can be seen to have established themselves on the walls of the building.

THE HOSPITAL 1893 32216

THE HOSPITAL 1921 70406

THE MUSEUM 1896 37309

Founded in 1847, Ipswich's museum was very much aimed at educating the working classes. In 1881, this new museum, designed by Horace Cheston, was built in the High Street.

THE WALK c1955 118030

This attractive pedestrian precinct is just off Tavern Street. Although the feel is Tudor, the straightness of the lines says otherwise. The Walk was actually built in the 1930s.

WOLSEY GATE AND ST PETER'S CHURCH 1893 32218
This brick gateway, which dates back to the 1520s, is all that stands of a scheme by Cardinal Wolsey to build a college in Ipswich. In fact the whole project was scarcely begun before Wolsey fell from grace.

WESTGATE STREET 1893 32201
The presence of tramlines and horse-drawn
carriages is not enough to deter pedestrians
from walking along the middle of the road.
This view looks eastwards along Westgate
Street, with the Cornhill in the distance; the
richly decorated town hall and post office peer
over the rooftops to the left.

THE TOWN HALL AND THE POST OFFICE 1896 37307

These two imposing buildings stand on Cornhill. On the left is the Post Office, built just five years previously, with its four statues representing Industry, Electricity, Steam and Commerce. To the right is the Italianate-style town hall, erected in 1867.

THE TOWN HALL c1955 118053

It is some sixty years after photograph No 37307, and while the fabric, and indeed usage, of the buildings remains pretty much the same, gas lamps have given way to electric street lights and power lines - and of course the ubiquitous motor car is making its presence felt.

THE TOWN HALL 1896 37308
This photograph lets us have a closer look at the Venetian-style town hall standing on Cornhill. The four figures below the clock represent Commerce, Agriculture, Learning and Justice.

THE WHITE HORSE 1893 32202
This view looks west along Tavern Street, with Cornhill in the distance. On the right-hand side is the unassuming Georgian facade of the Great White Horse Hotel, which actually hides a much older building; in its time it has played host to Charles Dickens, George II, Louis XVIII and Lord Nelson, who in 1800 was High Steward of Ipswich.

TAVERN STREET c1955 118036

It is over sixty years after photograph No 32202, and the Great White Horse Hotel has acquired stone cladding, several signs and a set of traffic lights. Strangely, the buildings on the left look more authentically old than they did in 1893!

TAVERN STREET 1896 37306

We are looking east along Tavern Street from Cornhill. On the left is the red brick and stone Lloyds Bank building, with its fretted skyline, while to the right is the neo-classical Post Office, built in 1881.

ST MARGARET'S CHURCH 1893 32220
Dating from the 15th century, St Margaret's church is regarded as the finest church in Ipswich. The exterior is richly decorated with stone and flint, while inside stands a monument to Sir Edmund Withipoll, who built nearby Christchurch Mansion.

OLD HOUSES, ST MARGARET'S PLAIN c1955 I18045
This group of Tudor houses was originally plastered, and before a road-widening scheme in 1931, three gables stood across the St Margaret's Plain end. The timberwork was exposed as part of the reconstruction after much of the building was demolished.

WESTGATE STREET 1893 32200
The name of the street harks back to the
days of the medieval walled town. The
gate itself was demolished in 1781.

THE CORN EXCHANGE 1893 32203
Built in 1882, the Corn Exchange continued in
use as such right up until 1972. Back in the days
when taking a picture involved a large and
unwieldy camera and tripod, a photographer
tended to attract a good deal of attention, but at
least there appear to be plenty of people to hand
willing to co-operate.

ST PETER'S STREET c1955 I18022

Here we see the tell-tale power lines which show that trolley buses are still operating. The first ones started running in 1923, and carried on until 1963. In the background is St Peter's church, close to which is Wolsey's Gate, all that remains of Cardinal Wolsey's efforts to build a great college of secular canons.

ST LAWRENCE STREET 1921 70389
This view looks northwards towards Tavern Street, with St Lawrence's church on the left; peering over the rooftops in the background is the unmistakable spire of St Mary-le-Tower.

FORE STREET 1893 32206
Clearly the photographer taking this picture caused a
major stir when he set up his hefty camera and tripod
in the street. And whilst some people know they need
to stand still for the slow exposure, not all of the
children seem to have the will power!

MAJOR'S CORNER c1955 I18033

Trolley buses were still operating in Ipswich when this photo was taken, as we can see from the overhead power lines. With traffic lights in the middle of the junction at Major's Corner, and pedestrian activity reasonably busy, where, one wonders, is all the traffic?

ELECTRIC HOUSE AND THE CAR PARK c1955 I18044

Electricity has played a great part in transport in Ipswich throughout the first half of the 20th century, first with trams, and then with the trolley buses. But the writing was certainly on the wall, judging from this jam-packed car park.

CHRISTCHURCH MANSION 1893 32217

Built on the site of the 12th-century priory of the Holy Trinity, this marvellous Tudor country house almost became a housing estate in the late 19th century. The Cobbold brewing family bought the building and then presented it to the town, thus enabling us to continue to enjoy this monument to gracious living.

CHRISTCHURCH PARK 1921 70405

A monument to Queen Victoria stands in the park in front of the 16th-century Christchurch Mansion. Its very Dutch-looking curved and pedimented gables came when the house was rebuilt after fire destroyed the upper storey in 1674. When Daniel Defoe visited Ipswich in 1722, he commented on how many townsfolk used the park, likening its popularity to that of Kensington Gardens.

THE GRAMMAR SCHOOL AND THE UPPER ARBORETUM 1921 70396
Ipswich's Grammar School was founded in the beginning of the 15th century. This particular building, designed
by Christopher Fleury, was built in what was then the outskirts of town, in the mid 19th century.

THE UPPER ARBORETUM 1921 70397
Here we see the beautiful ornamental gardens and the ornate drinking fountain in the arboretum adjoining the
Grammar School.

THE LOWER ARBORETUM 1893 32215
The Arboretum, adjacent to Christchurch Park, still survives, over a hundred years after this photograph was taken. These youngsters have stopped playing just long enough to stand still for the photographer.

FROM STOKE HILL 1893 32198
The railway arrived in Ipswich in 1846, and very quickly had an impact on industry and commerce. In 1860, a new station was opened at the north end of the tunnel through Stoke Hill, which then enabled the railway to be continued to Bury St Edmunds and Norwich.

THE DOCKS 1893 32208
Ipswich, at the head of the Orwell Estuary, has been a
major port for centuries. When this picture was taken,
the port was starting to enjoy commercial success after
a long period of decline.

ST PETER'S DOCK 1921 70411
Sailing barges are tied up in the Wet Dock, the non-tidal part
of the port of Ipswich. Adjacent to the dock are large
warehouses, including that of Cranfields, who along with
Pauls owned their own large fleets of barges.

THE LOCK GATES 1921 70413

A sailing barge negotiates the lock gates. The Wet Dock was constructed between 1839 and 1842, and at the time it was the most revolutionary and the biggest of its kind in the country.

THE DOCK ENTRANCE c1955 I18050

What makes the Wet Dock so useful is that it is a non-tidal section of the port. Water in the dock is held at a constant level by the lock gates.

THE DOCKS 1921 70412

THE DOCKS 1921
Sailing barges are moored on the river. Vessels like these were very much the mainstay of trade along the east coast, although by the time this photograph was taken, their days were certainly numbered.

THE PROMENADE 1893
This is a somewhat staged family photograph. This tree-lined avenue, which ran alongside the New Cut - the channel taking vessels from the river to the Wet Dock - was a favourite walk for the townsfolk of Ipswich. It was lost to further development of the docks.

THE PROMENADE 1893 32210

THE DOCKS 1921 70415
The old and new come together in this post World War I photograph, with a steamer in the foreground, and a sailing ship in the distance.

ON THE RIVER ORWELL 1909 61993
A sailing barge makes its way along the Orwell, with lush wooded hillsides coming down to meet the broad tidal mudflats at the water's edge.

HOG ISLAND 1921 70416
The name Hog Island has faded into history, although it lives on as a number of locations in New England.

HOG ISLAND 1921 70417
Once a popular riverside haunt for the locals, Hog Island is now known as Piper's Vale, and is more remarkable today as the north-eastern end of the Orwell Bridge.

THE DOCKS c1955 I18049
East Anglia has a long tradition for growing malting
barley, and Ipswich had a number of maltings. R & W
Paul's was right on the dockside.

THE POWER STATION c1955 118020
A 20th-century means of producing power shares the banks of the Orwell with vessels which harness one of the oldest forms of power. With shallow mudflats along the banks of the tidal Orwell estuary, moored sailing boats end up on their keels twice a day.

THE RIVER ORWELL 1921 70414
A sailing barge makes its way past a moored steamer. Outside the Wet Dock, tidal moorings were built for larger ships.

THE RIVER ORWELL AND SS 'NORFOLK' 1904 51246
Paddle steamers like this one used to operate along the East Coast, running pleasure trips to places like Felixstowe and Harwich. In the background are the masts of cargo ships.

THE RIVER ORWELL, IPSWICH STEAM BOATS 1921 70410
Paddle steamers provided pleasure trips and a bus service of sorts out to the coastal ports of Harwich and Felixstowe. Peering above the SS Suffolk are the tell-tale signs of Ipswich's malting industry.

SS 'SUFFOLK' 1896 37315

Looking at the lifeboat hanging from the davits (presumably there was one on the other side), one is tempted to wonder whether they would have been sufficient to cope in an emergency if this paddle steamer was fully laden. Up until the inquiry which followed the 'Titanic' disaster in 1912, lifeboat capacity on steamers was based on the ship's tonnage rather than the actual number of people carried.

ON THE GIPPING 1894 34817

Upstream from the docks, the river which flows through Ipswich is called the Gipping (hence the Saxon origins of the town's name - Gippeswic). Clearly, the prospects for rowing here look good.

ON THE GIPPING 1893 32209
This is a picture of tranquillity perhaps, but the Gipping was effectively a canal with a tow path, made to assist the carriage of goods upstream as far as Stowmarket.

BARKING TYE
The Shepherd 1934 86420
A between-the-wars picture of pastoral tranquillity. The only slightly odd element of the photograph is the shepherd himself - the suit and hat do not quite fit the stereotyped image!

HADLEIGH, THE GUILDHALL 1922 71975

Timbers this close together were not required for structural integrity: rather, they were a sign of opulence. Hadleigh's 15th-century Guildhall, with its two overhanging upper storeys, remains as a reminder of the huge wealth generated by the medieval wool trade.

HADLEIGH, ST MARY'S CHURCH 1922 71972

St Mary's, one of the largest in Suffolk, is not a typical Suffolk wool church, and has an elegant lead spire. Inside is the 600-year-old Angelus Bell, one of the oldest in the country, which is inscribed 'Ave Maria Gracia Plena Dominus Tecum'. Perhaps the man who made the bell had other things on his mind when it came to putting in the inscription, as he forgot to invert the words laterally in the mould, and they appear backwards on the finished article!

HADLEIGH, THE BRIDGE 1922 71979

This is the three-arched red brick medieval bridge over the River Brett at Hadleigh. King Guthrum, the first Danish king of East Anglia, had a palace at Hadleigh, and it is reputed that he is buried in the church.

HADLEIGH, OLD HOUSES IN THE HIGH STREET 1922 71970

These are 17th-century buildings. The Coffee Tavern came into being around thirty years previously - it was an attempt to provide people with an alternative to nearby public houses.

HADLEIGH, THE DEANERY TOWER 1922 71976

HADLEIGH
The Deanery Tower 1922
When the Deanery Tower was built in the latter part of the 15th century by Suffolk's Archdeacon, William Pykenham, it was supposed that it would be the gateway to a palace. But Pykenham's death put paid to further building. It is nevertheless a fine example of 15th-century brickwork.

SHOTLEY GATE
The Village c1955
Shotley Gate, at the very end of the Shotley Peninsula, was home to the former HMS 'Ganges', the Royal Navy's training school. This shore establishment gave its young recruits a stiff taste of discipline to fit them for their careers in the Navy. Each boy would be required to climb the 150ft high mast from HMS 'Cordelia', and every year, cadets at the passing-out ceremony had to climb the rigging, the pride of place going to the 'button boy', who perched on the eleven-inch diameter top of the mast.

SHOTLEY GATE, THE VILLAGE c1955 S581011

PIN MILL, THE BUTT AND OYSTER 1909   62001
The Butt and Oyster is probably the most well-known pub on the East Coast, at Pin Mill, on the River Orwell. Across the river from here is Orwell Park, in the 18th century the home of 'Old Grog' - Admiral Vernon. It was he who won sailors their daily ration of grog - rum and water.

PIN MILL, THE RIVER 1909 61998
A sailing boat on the River Orwell - the pub here has long been a favourite with the yachting fraternity.

PIN MILL, THE RIVER 1909 62000
This is the same yachtsman as in photograph No 61998, clearly there to add an extra dynamic to the photographs (note that he is looking underneath the boom, and the boat is actually moored).

PIN MILL, THE INN SIGN c1960 P370027
Here we see a close-up of the sign for the Butt and Oyster pub at Pin Mill. Although these days it is very much a yachtsman's haunt, Pin Mill used to see larger boats and barges lying up here, either for repairs or to offload goods.

PIN MILL, THE BOATYARD c1960 P370004

PIN MILL
The Boatyard c1960
We are looking back from the Butt and
Oyster pub towards the boatyard and
sailing club. A good deal of boat
building and repairing used to go on
here, but by now the main industry has
gone, and the cottages in the area are
more likely to be holiday homes.

◆

FRESTON TOWER 1893
Coastal Suffolk might not be the first
place you would think of for a
skyscraper, but the charming Tudor
redbrick folly Freston Tower could fit
the bill, albeit in a scaled-down manner.
It was probably built by prominent
Ipswich merchant Thomas Gooding
around 1550 as a study for his daughter.

FRESTON TOWER 1893 32233

WOOLVERSTONE HALL C1960 W443001
Built in the latter part of the 18th century, Woolverstone Hall was for many years the seat of the Berners family before it was taken over for use as a school.

ON THE ORWELL, THE CAT HOUSE 1893 32234
Built a hundred years prior to this photograph, this quaint Gothic cottage is named after the white cat painted in the window which overlooks the Orwell. Local legend has it that a stuffed white cat was placed in the window to signal that the coast was clear for smugglers coming ashore.

THE RIVER ORWELL FROM FRESTON PARK 1909 61997
Here we see a sailing boat on the edge of the Orwell below Freston Park. The Royal Harwich Yacht Club is not far away, along with a boatyard and the quaint cottage called the Cat House.

TRIMLEY, THE VILLAGE AND THE CHURCH 1899 43248
Trimley St Mary and Trimley St Martin lie just outside Felixstowe.

TRIMLEY, THE VILLAGE 1899 43250
The road here, rutted from the passage of many carriage wheels, is the main road from Felixstowe to Ipswich.

WALTON
The Village 1899 43246
Walton is now part of the suburbs of Felixstowe, but a
hundred years ago it was very much a village in its own
right, with the occasional pony and trap the only
concession to heavy traffic!

FELIXSTOWE, THE BEACH 1893 32231
It is a clear and sunny day, but very few people are on the beach. Felixstowe developed as a resort after the Empress of Germany stayed here in 1891.

WALTON, THE VILLAGE 1899 43245
A workman pauses from his digging - most likely connected with the gas street-lamp - while the photographer captures this street scene on the outskirts of Felixstowe.

WALDRINGFIELD, THE CLUB HOUSE AND THE BEACH c1960 W438045
Waldringfield is very much the place for yacht sailors, with its thriving boatyard, yacht club and pub. It is all here because this point along the River Deben has a steep shingle bank upon which boats can be landed or launched at any state of the tide.

WOODBRIDGE, THE PROMENADE 1925 78746
Relaxation is the name of the game, even without any serenading from the bandstand. These ladies are totally absorbed in their newspapers. Further along, other holidaymakers take in a bit more of what is going on around them.

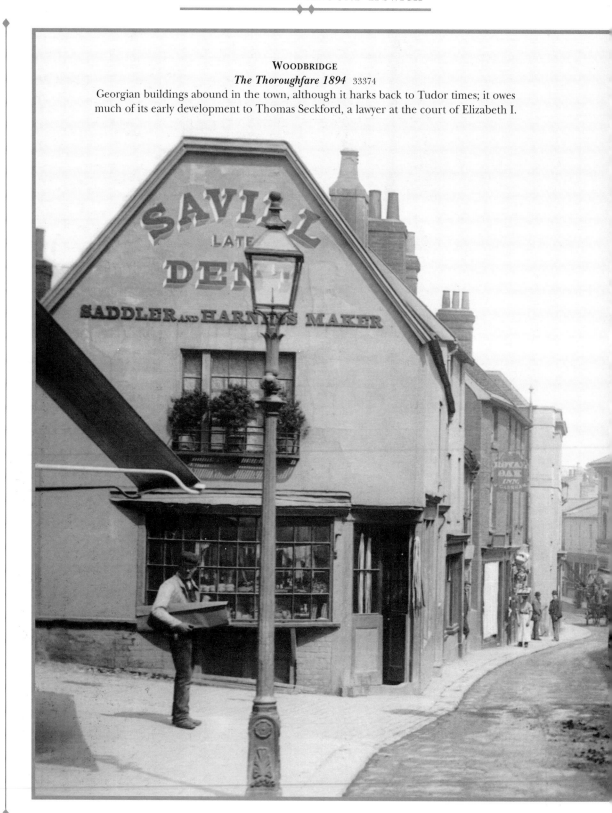

WOODBRIDGE
The Thoroughfare 1894 33374
Georgian buildings abound in the town, although it harks back to Tudor times; it owes much of its early development to Thomas Seckford, a lawyer at the court of Elizabeth I.

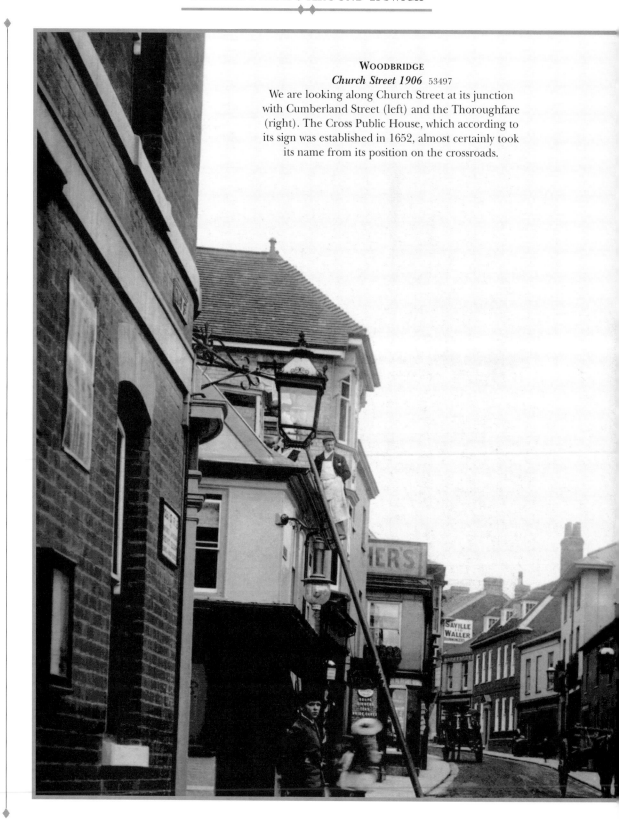

WOODBRIDGE
Church Street 1906 53497
We are looking along Church Street at its junction
with Cumberland Street (left) and the Thoroughfare
(right). The Cross Public House, which according to
its sign was established in 1652, almost certainly took
its name from its position on the crossroads.

WOODBRIDGE
The River Bank 1898 42772
This group of children and their parents
or nannies is enjoying the sun and fresh
air on the bank of the River Deben.

MELTON, STATION ROAD c1965 M268021
A quiet village on the outskirts of Woodbridge, maybe, but the sign on the pub is a reminder of the concentration of military bases in East Anglia at the height of the Cold War, with the radar station at Bawdsey and two US Air Force bases all within five miles of here.

MELTON, HIGH STREET c1955 M268001
Typical 1950s fashions are apparent in this photograph, with long overcoats the norm for a chilly day. The advertising above the shoe shop on the left shows that some favourite products have been around for generations.

Index

Frith Book Co Titles

Frith Book Company publish over a 100 new titles each year. For latest catalogue please contact Frith Book Co.

Town Books 96pp, 100 photos. County and Themed Books 128pp, 150 photos
(unless specified) All titles hardback laminated case and jacket
except those indicated pb (paperback)

Around Barnstaple	1-85937-084-5	£12.99
Around Blackpool	1-85937-049-7	£12.99
Around Bognor Regis	1-85937-055-1	£12.99
Around Bristol	1-85937-050-0	£12.99
Around Cambridge	1-85937-092-6	£12.99
Cheshire	1-85937-045-4	£14.99
Around Chester	1-85937-090-X	£12.99
Around Chesterfield	1-85937-071-3	£12.99
Around Chichester	1-85937-089-6	£12.99
Cornwall	1-85937-054-3	£14.99
Cotswolds	1-85937-099-3	£14.99
Around Derby	1-85937-046-2	£12.99
Devon	1-85937-052-7	£14.99
Dorset	1-85937-075-6	£14.99
Dorset Coast	1-85937-062-4	£14.99
Around Dublin	1-85937-058-6	£12.99
East Anglia	1-85937-059-4	£14.99
Around Eastbourne	1-85937-061-6	£12.99
English Castles	1-85937-078-0	£14.99
Around Falmouth	1-85937-066-7	£12.99
Hampshire	1-85937-064-0	£14.99
Isle of Man	1-85937-065-9	£14.99
Around Maidstone	1-85937-056-X	£12.99
North Yorkshire	1-85937-048-9	£14.99
Around Nottingham	1-85937-060-8	£12.99
Around Penzance	1-85937-069-1	£12.99
Around Reading	1-85937-087-X	£12.99
Around St Ives	1-85937-068-3	£12.99
Around Salisbury	1-85937-091-8	£12.99
Around Scarborough	1-85937-104-3	£12.99
Scottish Castles	1-85937-077-2	£14.99
Around Sevenoaks and Tonbridge	1-85937-057-8	£12.99

Sheffield and S Yorkshire	1-85937-070-5	£14.99
Shropshire	1-85937-083-7	£14.99
Staffordshire	1-85937-047-0 (96pp)	£12.99
Suffolk	1-85937-074-8	£14.99
Surrey	1-85937-081-0	£14.99
Around Torbay	1-85937-063-2	£12.99
Wiltshire	1-85937-053-5	£14.99
Around Bakewell	1-85937-113-2	£12.99
Around Bournemouth	1-85937-067-5	£12.99
Cambridgeshire	1-85937-086-1	£14.99
Essex	1-85937-082-9	£14.99
Around Great Yarmouth	1-85937-085-3	£12.99
Hertfordshire	1-85937-079-9	£14.99
Isle of Wight	1-85937-114-0	£14.99
Around Lincoln	1-85937-111-6	£12.99
Oxfordshire	1-85937-076-4	£14.99
Around Shrewsbury	1-85937-110-8	£12.99
South Devon Coast	1-85937-107-8	£14.99
Around Stratford upon Avon	1-85937-098-5	£12.99
West Midlands	1-85937-109-4	£14.99

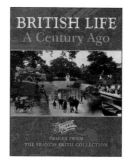

British Life A Century Ago
246 x 189mm
144pp, hardback.
Black and white
Lavishly illustrated with photos
from the turn of the century,
and with extensive commentary.
It offers a unique insight into
the social history and heritage
of bygone Britain.

1-85937-103-5 £17.99

Available from your local bookshop or from the publisher

Frith Book Co Titles Available in 2000

Around Bath	1-85937-097-7	£12.99	Mar
County Durham	1-85937-123-x	£14.99	Mar
Cumbria	1-85937-101-9	£14.99	Mar
Down the Thames	1-85937-121-3	£14.99	Mar
Around Exeter	1-85937-126-4	£12.99	Mar
Greater Manchester	1-85937-108-6	£14.99	Mar
Around Guildford	1-85937-117-5	£12.99	Mar
Around Harrogate	1-85937-112-4	£12.99	Mar
Around Leicester	1-85937-073-x	£12.99	Mar
Around Liverpool	1-85937-051-9	£12.99	Mar
Around Newark	1-85937-105-1	£12.99	Mar
Northumberland and Tyne & Wear			
	1-85937-072-1	£14.99	Mar
Around Oxford	1-85937-096-9	£12.99	Mar
Around Plymouth	1-85937-119-1	£12.99	Mar
Around Southport	1-85937-106-x	£12.99	Mar
Welsh Castles	1-85937-120-5	£14.99	Mar
Around Belfast	1-85937-094-2	£12.99	Apr
Canals and Waterways	1-85937-129-9	£17.99	Apr
Down the Severn	1-85937-118-3	£14.99	Apr
East Sussex	1-85937-130-2	£14.99	Apr
Exmoor	1-85937-132-9	£14.99	Apr
Gloucestershire	1-85937-102-7	£14.99	Apr
Around Horsham	1-85937-127-2	£12.99	Apr
Around Ipswich	1-85937-133-7	£12.99	Apr
Ireland (pb)	1-85937-181-7	£9.99	Apr
Kent Living Memories	1-85937-125-6	£14.99	Apr
London (pb)	1-85937-183-3	£9.99	Apr
New Forest	1-85937-128-0	£14.99	Apr
Scotland (pb)	1-85937-182-5	£9.99	Apr
Around Southampton	1-85937-088-8	£12.99	Apr
Stone Circles & Ancient Monuments			
	1-85937-143-4	£17.99	Apr
Sussex (pb)	1-85937-184-1	£9.99	Apr
Colchester (pb)	1-85937-188-4	£8.99	May
County Maps of Britain			
	1-85937-156-6 (192pp)	£19.99	May
Leicestershire (pb)	1-85937-185-x	£9.99	May

Lincolnshire	1-85937-135-3	£14.99	May
Around Newquay	1-85937-140-x	£12.99	May
Nottinghamshire (pb)	1-85937-187-6	£9.99	May
Redhill to Reigate	1-85937-137-x	£12.99	May
Victorian & Edwardian Yorkshire			
	1-85937-154-x	£14.99	May
Around Winchester	1-85937-139-6	£12.99	May
Yorkshire (pb)	1-85937-186-8	£9.99	May
Berkshire (pb)	1-85937-191-4	£9.99	Jun
Brighton (pb)	1-85937-192-2	£8.99	Jun
Dartmoor	1-85937-145-0	£14.99	Jun
East London	1-85937-080-2	£14.99	Jun
Glasgow (pb)	1-85937-190-6	£8.99	Jun
Kent (pb)	1-85937-189-2	£9.99	Jun
Victorian & Edwardian Kent			
	1-85937-149-3	£14.99	Jun
North Devon Coast	1-85937-146-9	£14.99	Jun
Peak District	1-85937-100-0	£14.99	Jun
Around Truro	1-85937-147-7	£12.99	Jun
Victorian & Edwardian Maritime Album			
	1-85937-144-2	£17.99	Jun
West Sussex	1-85937-148-5	£14.99	Jun
Churches of Berkshire	1-85937-170-1	£17.99	Jul
Churches of Dorset	1-85937-172-8	£17.99	Jul
Churches of Hampshire	1-85937-207-4	£17.99	Jul
Churches of Wiltshire	1-85937-171-x	£17.99	Jul
Derbyshire (pb)	1-85937-196-5	£9.99	Jul
Edinburgh (pb)	1-85937-193-0	£8.99	Jul
Herefordshire	1-85937-174-4	£14.99	Jul
Norwich (pb)	1-85937-194-9	£8.99	Jul
Ports and Harbours	1-85937-208-2	£17.99	Jul
Somerset and Avon	1-85937-153-1	£14.99	Jul
South Devon Living Memories			
	1-85937-168-x	£14.99	Jul
Warwickshire (pb)	1-85937-203-1	£9.99	Jul
Worcestershire	1-85937-152-3	£14.99	Jul
Yorkshire Living Memories			
	1-85937-166-3	£14.99	Jul

FRITH PRODUCTS & SERVICES

Francis Frith would doubtless be pleased to know that the pioneering publishing venture he started in 1860 still continues today. More than a hundred and thirty years later, The Francis Frith Collection continues in the same innovative tradition and is now one of the foremost publishers of vintage photographs in the world. Some of the current activities include:

Interior Decoration

Today Frith's photographs can be seen framed and as giant wall murals in thousands of pubs, restaurants, hotels, banks, retail stores and other public buildings throughout the country. In every case they enhance the unique local atmosphere of the places they depict and provide reminders of gentler days in an increasingly busy and frenetic world.

Product Promotions

Frith products have been used by many major companies to promote the sales of their own products or to reinforce their own history and heritage. Brands include Hovis bread, Courage beers, Scots Porage Oats, Colman's mustard, Cadbury's foods, Mellow Birds coffee, Dunhill pipe tobacco, Guinness, and Bulmer's Cider.

Genealogy and Family History

As the interest in family history and roots grows world-wide, more and more people are turning to Frith's photographs of Great Britain for images of the towns, villages and streets where their ancestors lived; and, of course, photographs of the churches and chapels where their ancestors were christened, married and buried are an essential part of every genealogy tree and family album.

A series of easy-to-use CD Roms is planned for publication, and an increasing number of Frith photographs will be able to be viewed on specialist genealogy sites. A growing range of Frith books will be available on CD.

The Internet

Already thousands of Frith photographs can be viewed and purchased on the internet. By the end of the year 2000 some 60,000 Frith photographs will be available on the internet. The number of sites is constantly expanding, each focussing on different products and services from the Collection.

Some of the sites are listed below.

www.townpages.co.uk
www.icollector.com
www.barclaysquare.co.uk
www.cornwall-online.co.uk

For background information on the Collection look at the three following sites:

www.francisfrith.com
www.francisfrith.co.uk
www.frithbook.co.uk

Frith Products

All Frith photographs are available Framed or just as Mounted Prints, and can be ordered from the address below. From time to time other products - Address Books, Calendars, Table Mats, etc - are available.

For further information:
if you would like further information on any of the above aspects of the Frith business please contact us at the address below:
The Francis Frith Collection,
Frith's Barn, Teffont, Salisbury, Wiltshire,
England SP3 5QP.
Tel: +44 (0)1722 716 376 Fax: +44 (0)1722 716 881   Email: uksales@francisfrith.com

---

To receive your FREE Mounted Print

Mounted Print
Overall size 14 x 11 inches

Cut out this Voucher and return it with your remittance for £1.50 to cover postage and handling. Choose any photograph included in this book. Your SEPIA print will be A4 in size, and mounted in a cream mount with burgundy rule lines, overall size 14 x 11 inches.

Order additional Mounted Prints at HALF PRICE (only £7.49 each*)

If there are further pictures you would like to order, possibly as gifts for friends and family, acquire them at half price (no additional postage and handling required).

Have your Mounted Prints framed*

For an additional £14.95 per print you can have your chosen Mounted Print framed in an elegant polished wood and gilt moulding, overall size 16 x 13 inches (no additional postage and handling required).

> *** IMPORTANT!**
> These special prices are only available if ordered using the original voucher on this page (no copies permitted) and at the same time as your free Mounted Print, for delivery to the same address

Frith Collectors' Guild

From time to time we publish a magazine of news and stories about Frith photographs and further special offers of Frith products. If you would like 12 months FREE membership, please return this form.

Send completed forms to:
The Francis Frith Collection, Frith's Barn, Teffont, Salisbury, Wiltshire SP3 5QP

Voucher for FREE and Reduced Price Frith Prints

Picture no.	Page number	Qty	Mounted @ £7.49	Framed + £14.95	Total Cost
		1	**Free of charge***	£	£
			£7.49	£	£
			£7.49	£	£
			£7.49	£	£
			£7.49	£	£
			£7.49	£	£
			* Post & handling		£1.50

Book Title . . . .   **Total Order Cost**   £

Please do not photocopy this voucher. Only the original is valid, so please cut it out and return it to us.

I enclose a cheque / postal order for £ . . . .
made payable to 'The Francis Frith Collection'
OR please debit my Mastercard / Visa / Switch / Amex card

Number . . . .

Expires . . . . Signature . . . .

Name Mr/Mrs/Ms . . . .

Address . . . .

. . . .

. . . .

. . . .

. . . . Postcode . . . .

Daytime Tel No . . . .   Valid to 31/12/01

The Francis Frith Collectors' Guild

Please enrol me as a member for 12 months free of charge.

Name Mr/Mrs/Ms . . . .

Address . . . .

. . . .

. . . .

. . . . Postcode . . . .

Free Print - see overleaf